Living the Simple RV Life

www.yellowcatbooks.com

• ALSO BY SUNNY SKYE

The Truth About the RV Life

RVing with Pets

RV Boondocking Basics

Tales of a Campground Host

• FOR •

My Fellow Nomads

Contents

Introduction

Are you wishing for a better and simpler life where you can spend each day as you wish? RV expert Sunny Skye shows you how you can do exactly this, even if you don't have much money.

Sunny has been RVing since she was a kid, and she'll show you how to leave the American Dream behind for a more realistic and fulfilling way to live—a simpler and less stressful life.

This book is not just filled with good advice, but also offers hope to anyone who wants to live on the road or close to nature but doesn't have the money or know how to get started.

This book covers the following topics:

- The Simple RV Life
- Do You Have What it Takes to Full-Time?
- Is This Lifestyle for You?
- How Can You Tell if You'll Succeed as an RVer?
- Leaving Your Options Open/Know Thyself
- Fear
- Some Benefits of the RV Life

- Some Drawbacks of the RV Life
- How to Get Started
- Getting Free of Stuff
- Organization
- Getting a Rig
- Picking a Home Base
- Life on the Road
- Is RVing Physically Difficult?
- Getting Sick or Injured
- Work and Money
- Where Can I Park?
- Will I Be Safe?
- On Loneliness and Civilization
- Traveling with Pets
- Communications and The Internet
- Weather
- Food and Water
- Power
- Staying Clean
- Having an Exit Plan

If you enjoy this book, you'll also like *Sunny's Tales of a Campground Host, RVing with Pets, RV Boondocking Basics,* and *The Truth about the RV Life*.

Preface

Were you born with a bit of gypsy blood, yearning for the day you can just chuck it all and be free? Do you look wistfully at passing travelers in their RVs, wishing you could live life on the road?

Does it somehow seem like an impossible dream, one you'll have to put off until you can retire, though by then you suspect you may be too old to really enjoy it? Or maybe you're already retired, but just can't figure out if it's the right choice or not—or maybe you don't think you can afford it.

An entire subculture exists in North America of people who live full-time in their RVs, vehicles that range from vans and tiny camp trailers to the biggest 40-foot diesel pushers (those huge bus-like RVs), with everything imaginable in between.

You may not be aware of the large number of people who live the RV lifestyle, as the full-time RV subculture is a relatively unobtrusive one, one you may be aware of only when you stumble across an RVer's blog on the internet or pass a distant wagon circle of rigs out in the desert.

But a subculture it is, one with an estimated two million people who RV full-time, and many more who do it part-time. And there's really no reason you can't join them, if you want. You can live the simple RV life, and without a lot of money.

Simplicity

Pick up a typical RV magazine and you'll see full-color lavish ads for huge RV developments in places where the retired like to spend their winters—usually in Florida or the American Southwest. You'll see photos with big expensive RVs all lined up in a row in some beautiful RV park with long lists of the amenities available, such as cable TV, pools, casinos, golf courses, etc.

This is one type of RVing, but one I'll pretty much steer clear of in this book, as it can get expensive and is somewhat the same as having a big expensive house, except on wheels, and you might as well be back in suburbia, except the neighbors come and go more often.

Some of those RVs actually cost more than the average house and defy anyone's definition of simplicity. This book will focus instead on how to live in a smaller space and with a modest pocketbook, which seems to be more the norm these days than not. So, if you're wanting to go the big Class A RV route, this book may not be that much help to you, as I'll focus more on the simple lifestyle.

Do You Have the Nomad Gene?

Some consider full-timing in an RV to be an alternate reality, and in a way, it is. But it's a reality that's much closer to the life our nomadic ancestors once lived. We may not want to return to the hardships humans encountered as hunter-gatherers, but we can return to the lifestyle that many of us seem to still have in our genes.

Nomadism served the human race well in early times, as it distributed the population across areas with resources and also ensured a healthy gene pool. Wild animals often range (not the same as migrating) across wide areas, which provides the same benefit. And some evidence exists that levels of dopamine production in the brain may determine why some are more exploratory and curious by nature than others.

Whatever accounts for it, more people than you might guess have the desire to wander, some wanting nothing to do with a permanent home at all, selling everything they own and devoting their lives to seeing new places. Some take early retirement, sell out, and go spend their kids' inheritances.

But lest you think the majority of such types are retirees, that's not the case at all. Many nomads are younger people who realize the best time to travel is when they're young and physically fit. And they also figure out how to do it without having a bundle of money, or in some cases, hardly any money at all.

And recently, more and more people are choosing this lifestyle for economic reasons, then discovering they're well-suited to it and wish they'd done it sooner. They may have lost their homes and jobs and don't want to wait around to regain control of their lives, so they make do and hit the road, some living in their cars. Some of these are recent college graduates who discover their job prospects are slim, so they get a cheap RV and follow the seasonal or day-job circuit.

Should I Do This?

Those considering becoming a part of the full-time RV lifestyle always have a lot of questions, but sometimes the main question is whether or not they're doing the right thing.

You may not want to ask just anyone that question, as nomadic types tend to threaten the status quo, and those who value security will think you're off on an impossible quest. And of course, it's normal for you to also worry about hitting the road full time, especially before you realize how great the full-time RV life can be.

You have to know your own mind before you decide, and then you have to honor your decision. That's not to say you can't change your mind later. The average time for a full-timer to stay on the road seems to be about three or four years, from what I can tell from my research and talking to literally thousands of full-timers, so there may be a time when one wants to get off the road, but that's another matter entirely, one we'll cover later. And keep in mind that some happily RV for many many years.

For now, know yourself before making the commitment, especially if it involves selling real estate. We'll go into this in more detail later and discuss ways to know what you really want and need—it can be a conflicting decision. In any case, it's not a decision to make lightly.

Can I Do This?

We'll also explore whether or not you're the right personality type for this lifestyle and how you can do it financially.

It amazes me how many people tell me, "I wish I could take off and live in an RV like you do," yet when I tell them they can, they list all the reasons they can't.

Many of these are just excuses based in fear or from not really wanting to commit, but for those who really want to RV full-time, usually the main drawback is being in debt and wondering where they'll get money if they're not going to have a regular job.

These are obstacles that can be overcome, given time and dedication, but most people aren't serious when they say they wish they could RV. You must first determine if you really are the full-timer type, and if so, how to take the steps necessary to make your dreams come true. As with most things, the first and biggest step is making the commitment, but determination in seeing that decision through plays a big part, too.

It seems that the hardest part of living the RV life for many is plotting how to free yourself of your job and house and those encumbrances that hold you back, especially the mental and internal ones.

It can be truly scary breaking free of all the things that provide security, but RVers know that real security is doing what you want with your life, as happiness energizes your creativity and resourcefulness, enabling you to maximize your skills in ways you never thought possible. You can break out of the old familiar rut into a new exciting life. No, it's not a life without hardships, but what life is?

Making Great Memories

So, come along for the trip, and maybe you'll decide you want to make RVing your new lifestyle. And of course, nothing's forever, so you may decide at some point to go back to what RVer's call a "sticks and bricks," a permanent home where you can sit by the fireplace and recall all your fond memories of the good RV life.

Either way, you can't lose—whether you RV for a short time or for the rest of your life. It's something almost everyone should try, if just for the great memories.

The Simple RV Life

Just how does one know for sure that the RV life is for them?

Well, usually you just know, as typically this trait displays itself at a young age. For example, when I was a kid, I'd climb the sagebrush-covered hill behind our house and look off to the distant horizon, wondering what was out there, wanting nothing more than to go see.

I grew up on the edge of a small town in northwest Colorado, and I don't recall going anywhere more than an hour or two's drive from home until I was ten or so. But my family did spend a lot of time camping and exploring, and maybe it was being a local nomad that ingrained the desire in me to wander, because all I've ever wanted to do since then was explore.

Many of you are probably what I call local nomads, people who can't really travel like they want, so who instead explore locally, getting to know every road and ridge in their territory. Maybe it's that explorer gene.

If you're like this, it's a good sign you're RV material. And if you chomp at the bit wishing you could run away from home, and you spend lots of time looking at maps and travel books and websites, that's another pretty good indicator.

The simple RV life involves a kind of mindset—figuring out your own needs and how to provide them, learning to be self-sufficient (if you're not already so), becoming a good fixer of broken things and problem solver, not minding hardships (like cold and rain), and basically living close to nature.

Even if you have a big rig that provides many comforts, you're still living closer to nature than someone in a house, and this can create its own set of problems, as well as benefits.

There are as many ways to explore as there are people—some prefer to camp in the same place for a few weeks and others want to go some place new every day. Some are happy with a tent, and others want a 40-foot rig with all the amenities of a fine hotel.

The problem with living the simple RV life, always exploring, is captured in an old song: "The bear went over the mountain, to see what he could see. The other side of the mountain was all that he could see."

You get to the other side, and there's always another mountain off in the distance, and it never ends. It's something you just have to keep on doing, this exploration thing. That's why getting the right rig is important—if for nothing else, so you can afford the gas to go other places.

I believe that we humans aren't really all that far removed from our hunting and gathering ancestors, and those who pursue the RV lifestyle are not as apt to fit the mold society prefers.

Maybe the RV type is just too much of an independent thinker, plus we don't typically buy much stuff because we have nowhere to put it, so we're not good consumers. But be aware that, as an RVer, some will lump you in with vagrants and the destitute.

Keep in mind that I'm referring to the simple RVer, not to those in the big rigs who stay in campgrounds. They typically support local businesses more by eating out and playing golf and buying things, as they usually have places to put stuff. Like anything in this society, the more money you seem to have, the more red carpet treatment you'll receive by those wanting to part you from that money. And I say the more money you seem to have, as owning a big rig doesn't necessarily mean it's paid for.

More and more towns and counties are enacting laws preventing people in RVs from overnighting on streets and in empty lots, and you will occasionally run into those who don't want your business because they've stereotyped you, such as campgrounds who won't accept a rig over a certain age, no matter how well-kept it is. This tends to happen more in urban areas and is one reason people tend to head out West where there are fewer rules and more open spaces.

RVers tend to vote with their feet, and you can always just go some place where you're more welcome, if this happens to you. It's rare, but is just one more on the list of things to be aware of.

Perhaps the most successful RV mindset is the one where you let such things roll off your back like water on a duck. Life's too short to sweat it, so you happily move on to what you know will be a better place.

It's kind of like Lee Marvin in that old movie classic, "Paint Your Wagon" where he sings about being born under a ramblin' star, where "hell is in hello, and heaven's in goodbye again, I think it's time to go."

He would have for sure made a great RVer.

Do You Have What it Takes to Full-Time?

Just asking this question implies that there's maybe something wrong with those who choose not to full-time in an RV, but that's not really true. People have different values and needs, and not everyone enjoys the instability of the RV life. It's important that you determine if you're the type who likes to full-time before you make a commitment that you can't as easily get out of.

I have a friend who has a good job in management, but who spends all his time daydreaming about quitting his job and full-timing. He's old enough to retire, and he hates where he lives in the humid South. He once took a road trip around the West and now dreams of selling his house (which is paid for), buying an RV, and heading out into the sunset.

It's a dream many have, a dream tied to getting rid of onerous responsibilities—the nine to five job, the commute, the bills—well, you know the story, it all goes with the Great American Dream. We've all wished we could just get free of it somehow.

Another friend, who we'll call Dave, has the means to do exactly what he wants. He's not wealthy, but he's managed to save and do fairly well for himself. He calls me about once a week to discuss the possibilities—what kind of RV he should buy, whether he should sell his house or rent it, etc. etc. These questions seem to be kind of a revolving door for him—he'll make a decision, then go on to the next problem, until I'm sure he's finally ready to act.

Next thing I know, he's back to the beginning again, not sure if he should buy a Class A (the ones that look like buses) or a Class C (the ones that look like homes on a truck chassis) or a trailer, or if he should sell his house or rent it. He analyzes it all, but never acts. Then, after going through this process, he'll call, depressed and not sure if he should even be considering RVing or not.

I truly believe one should carefully examine all their options before leaping, but Dave has what's called "analysis paralysis." He lets his fears of the unknown stop him from proceeding in the direction he wants to go, then gets depressed because he's not doing what he really wants, but is instead letting his fears hold him back.

Does my friend have what it takes to full-time? I don't know, but I suspect he does. Once he makes the decision and follows through with it, I think he'll enjoy what he's doing and be happy for it. But living on the road does take a certain amount of gung-ho personality—you can't analyze everything to death but need to have faith in your own abilities to handle difficult situations. You have to be able to make decisions and be resourceful.

Is This Lifestyle for You?

Deciding to full-time is a major life decision, especially if you don't have the means to return to a sticks and bricks lifestyle. I usually advise people who haven't done much RVing to first downsize—get rid of everything they don't really need or want—then rent their house out or close it down for a few months and try the full-time lifestyle before committing to it fully. That way, it's much easier to return to your former life, should you decide the RV life is not for you.

But sometimes you don't have a choice. You may not be able to hold onto your house while you try things out, as you can't take off work that long or you just simply don't have the means to have an RV and a house both. Many have to sell their houses before they can buy an RV. And typically your employer won't just give you a few months off.

Some full-timers are living that lifestyle by necessity, not because they want to. The economy has pushed many from their homes onto the road, and some of these full-timers would much prefer living in a more stable environment. Do they have what it takes? Yes, but they'd rather not be doing it.

I believe a certain type of person loves full-timing, while others simply aren't cut out for it. There's certainly no honor lost in not enjoying the RV lifestyle, but many people have found this out after they've cut all their ties and wished they hadn't. As I mentioned before, the average full-timer lasts only three or four years, then returns to a house. But some have done it for twenty years or more and still love it and will quit only when they have no choice.

What kind of person best enjoys the RV life? I think those who are happy living this way generally have the following traits:

- Can easily adapt to different circumstances
- Tends not to take things too seriously
- Enjoys the outdoors and solitude
- Is good at problem solving
- Doesn't need external stimulation
- Doesn't need a lot of comforts and things
- Enjoys simplicity
- Is resourceful
- Doesn't sweat the small stuff

Some of these traits take awhile to develop, but I think the successful full-timer eventually finds that life is better without all the negative things we use to distract ourselves—things like too much television and overeating and mindless shopping.

Sitting in your camp chair watching a stunning sunset tends to make you forget that you're missing your favorite TV show (and many full-timers do bring their TVs along, so you don't necessarily have to go cold-turkey).

After awhile, you rediscover the joys of things like talking around a campfire, bird-watching, and a quiet walk around the lake with your dogs—those kinds of things become part of your life as never before, and it seems that full-timers tend to stop and smell the roses more.

So, how does this apply to you? Well, it's important in determining if you're the type of person who will be happy as an RVer. And when I say RVer, I'm not talking about camping. Campers go home after awhile, where full-time RVers don't, although they may spend time occasionally renting a house.

Are you the kind of person who likes to be outside a lot? Or would you prefer to go out for a couple of hours and then go home and kick back with a cup of coffee or hot chocolate? Either way, you might have the makings of a happy RVer. The key ingredient here is liking the outdoors.

We're each looking for a better way to live, and even if you're exploring this lifestyle from economic necessity, there's no reason you can't also improve your life as part of the deal. The RV life can be a good one, but you have to be sure you're suited to it, and not everyone is.

Think about it—what's not to like about waking up each day to a view others would pay lots of money for? And you can change that view whenever you want. You can live in a setting that would cost a fortune if you were to have a house there, although most of the places you'll be won't allow houses. Imagine living in or next to a national park, for example.

We all know there's a big difference between wishing and making a wish come true, and the simple RV life is within the reach of almost everyone who has the desire to make that wish happen.

I say almost, because there are, of course, exceptions, those who can't live in an RV no matter how much they want to, people with so many responsibilities that there's no way they could leave. But even many of those people can plan for the future when the kids are grown or they can eventually free themselves from whatever's holding them back.

Such cases aren't as common as you might think, and I doubt seriously if you're one of them. You may think you are, but most obstacles are simply challenges to be overcome. It may take longer than you wish, but it usually can be done.

How Can You Tell if You'll Succeed as an RV'er?

How can you tell if you'll succeed as an RVer without just going and doing it? It can be difficult to sell your rig and get back into a house, so you want to have a good feel for your ability to do this before starting. There are a number of ways to know, and the fact that you're reading this book is a good indicator that you'll succeed. But full-timing requires a special mindset, one we'll explore.

First, are you the kind of person who likes to camp? As I mentioned before, if you're RVing, you're typically outdoors a lot, and your propensity to enjoy this is critical to whether or not you're full-time material. If you like to be outside a lot, then that's a major indicator you'll be happy living in an RV.

Are you independent and like to solve your own problems? With RVing, your home is wherever you park, and typically, unless you stay in an RV park for some time (which can get expensive), your daily existence will revolve around where you happen to be and where you're going next.

And when you move a lot, you don't have neighbors or friends around to help solve problems, and you therefore need a good level of self-sufficiency. This is not a given, as some people choose to travel in groups, but even then, you're often on your own for the day by day things.

Do you enjoy solitude? Do you get easily bored? Boondocking, or camping without hookups, usually out in the backcountry, is most often accompanied by solitude. You may often be the only person around for miles.

At first, having lots of time to yourself will be awesome, but be prepared for boredom. Some people never get bored, and those are the truly self-sufficient types, but some do. Are you good at entertaining yourself? Do you go shopping a lot for entertainment?

Do you like to travel? If you're the homebody type, don't give up on RVing, as some RVers tend to stay in the same locales, moving as necessary but within that area. But a lot of RVers live the lifestyle because they want to get out and see new places. You'll probably be happier with this lifestyle if you're one of the latter.

Are you security minded? If you feel lost when traveling, or need the security of a house around you with daily routines, you may not like RVing, though even this mindset can be accommodated. RVers have routines just like everyone else, and their rig becomes their secure home, but if you need a real house, you may not be the RV type, at least not full-time.

Do you like change and challenges? The RV life is the definition of change, as you'll always be going someplace new, and even if it's back to a place you stayed before, it's still change. Some people have routes they follow with the seasons, which gives a sense of security, but nothing's ever the same, at least not like staying home.

Do you mind leaving your family and friends behind? This is a big consideration for many, but don't forget that often the RV life allows you to spend more time with your family than before, especially if they're scattered all over the country. You can travel to them and stay as long as you're welcome, which I guarantee will be a lot longer than if you were staying in their house. Parking in their driveway or even a nearby RV park gives the degree of separation that leads to better relations.

These are all factors to consider when choosing the RV life, especially if you won't have a fixed base to return to. But maybe the most important consideration is this: do you have an indomitable spirit? The full-time RVer tends to not easily get discouraged by day-to-day problems and just carries on anyway.

Leaving Your Options Open/Know Thyself

It's important to keep your options open if you're not sure about the RV life. If possible, don't sell your house, just rent it out, or even just try RVing for short periods of time.

If you find yourself eager to get back home, then maybe the full-time life isn't for you. There's certainly no honor lost in that, it just means that maybe you don't have the explorer gene.

If everyone was a nomad, who would stick around to provide grocery stores and gas stations for the wanderers? Everyone has a place, and knowing where you're happiest means knowing yourself. Part of knowing yourself is not mistaking your fears for what you really want.

For example, my friend Cass always wanted to go try out the RV life, but she never could quite make the necessary arrangements. She had friends who RVed, and she always sat in envy when they visited and told her about all the great places they'd been and things they'd seen.

Now, if ever there was someone who I would've predicted would make a great RVer, it was Cass. She was very outdoorsy and loved to bike and hike. She had retired fairly young and was active and curious and enjoyed meeting new people. But she also loved to garden, which became a hindrance to being a nomad.

Cass finally decided she would be an RVer. She wanted to experiment first to see how it went, so she rented a Class C RV to take a short trip to see how she liked it. I was excited for her and knew she would love it.

Well, she called to tell me she'd changed her mind, as she'd found out her aunt would be in town that weekend and she wanted to see her. That seemed like a good enough reason to me, and I thought little of it.

Well, Cass did this several times, renting an RV, then finding some reason to cancel at the last minute.

I have no idea how much money she lost doing this, as she would always rent one of those Class C's that you see tooling down the road with "Rent Me" on it. I know she lost her deposit fee more than once.

Cass finally told me she was afraid to go alone, and I accepted her explanation and tried to encourage her. She soon found a friend to go along, and the trip went well.

Not long after, she rented a Class C and actually went out alone, telling me she was finally facing her fears. I was happy for her, and she called me every day to tell me how the trip was going and also so someone would know of her whereabouts.

She seemed happy enough on the phone, but when Cass returned, she wasn't nearly as enthusiastic as I thought a happy RVer should be. She told me she really hadn't enjoyed it that much. I figured it was because she had gone alone. I encouraged her to not give up, thinking she really wanted to do this.

So, off she went again, but this time with another friend. When she finally returned, she told me she was happy to be home and had decided it just wasn't the life for her.

She hated all the roughing it that went with RVing—laundromats, not having all her cooking supplies (she's a gourmet chef), and the feeling she had of insecurity, even though she was sleeping inside a very secure vehicle. She hated having to look for places to camp and the unsettled feeling it all gave her. And she missed her garden.

Cass had learned something about herself—she wasn't afraid of RVing at all, she simply wasn't the RV type. She loved the security and spaciousness of having a house, and she wasn't happy being a wanderer.

What she had thought was fear was really dislike. She had tried to fit herself into a lifestyle that sounded glamorous to her, but she just wasn't that type.

Now Cass is happy being a host for her RVing friends, providing a place where they can come and take a break. She loves hearing their stories, but she especially likes hearing about any problems they've had, as it reaffirms her own happiness at being a nester.

In contrast to Cass is my friend Ron, who everyone said would hate being a full-time RVer.

Ron was a third-generation Bostonian, raised in a Victorian brownstone in the very urban section of Back Bay. His parents were artists, and Ron had hardly ever been out of the city when he decided he wanted to try out the RV life.

Ron had never even camped out, and, at the age of 45, he sold everything he owned and bought a small trailer to pull behind his new-to-him Toyota pickup.

His friends were somewhat horrified and mystified at this new direction, and most of them predicted he wouldn't last a month. Ron eventually lost touch with them, as they no longer had anything in common. He discovered the beauty of camping on the rugged beaches of Maine and gradually drifted on up into the cottage country of Ontario, Canada.

Ron worked from the road, writing web content and working only enough to support his very frugal lifestyle. When I met him at a farmer's market in Colorado, he'd been on the road for 15 years and had no desire to ever go back to his previous lifestyle.

He returned to Boston only to visit his parents, and he'd even managed to acquire a couple of rescued cats along the way, as well as to upgrade to a larger trailer and bigger pickup.

He seemed happy and well, and he told me he found the idea of living in a house depressing. He also told me he was allergic to cities.

He and Cass are both happy living in different worlds. Both had discovered what it took to make them so, and that knowledge was based on understanding themselves.

Fear

Don't let fear hold you back. Fear can keep us from harm if it's a reasonable fear, but if it's an unreasonable fear, it can make us do things that are counter to our own well- being.

For example, after getting my first trailer, I camped in the outback for 10 days before I decided I needed to unhook and go into town, which wasn't really that far away, just a few miles. I'd never unhooked a trailer before, and I didn't want to haul the trailer into town, so I just sat there.

I was completely out of food and nearly out of water before I decided I had to act. Come to find out, it took about five minutes to unhook and was incredibly easy. My fears were unreasonable and held me back. I was eating the last of my food—soup and crackers—when I could have been dining on a fresh salad and nice hot pizza.

It's good to experiment before you get out by yourself and while there are people around who can help you. Many people prefer campgrounds for this very reason—there's usually someone around who will help out if needed. This is fine, but if you want to boondock out in the backcountry, don't let your fears stop you.

Pulling a trailer can be very intimidating at first, and I'm sure every newbie can tell stories about how scared they were and how easy it turned out to be. It helps to read stories about mistakes others have made so you don't repeat them, and this is where the numerous RV forums come in handy.

You'll read about every mistake made under the sun and then some. If and when your turn comes, you'll have a better idea of how to handle things. Just don't let the mistakes others have made scare you into not trying it out. One very popular forum that covers many RVing topics is rv.net, which is hosted by Camping World.

One way to deal with potential problems is to get roadside service. But don't get lulled into thinking they will always rescue you, and be prepared to fend for yourself. For example, I once broke down in the little Colorado mountain town of Silverton. I had AAA service and wasn't a bit worried, thinking they would come and get me and tow my rig to a shop.

I was quickly informed that this was one of the few towns in the U.S. that they wouldn't cover because the nearest tow truck was 60 miles away over a steep mountain pass. Needless to say, I cancelled their service. Even the best of roadside services have times when they won't be there for you, even if it's just because of an inept call-center employee.

It's hard when you live so close to the edge financially that even a small error can sink you. Don't let that stop you, as such mistakes don't have to be made if you're aware, and in the meantime, keep working on how to create a financial buffer for yourself. But whatever you do, be aware that most fears are unfounded and the worst will almost never happen.

One way to really understand what you're getting into when you move into a recreational vehicle is to get on the internet and read as many RV blogs as you can. Many full-time RVers have blogs, and they enjoy giving daily updates on where they're at and what they're doing, as well as the problems they've encountered—and solutions.

Reading blogs will give you a very good insight into what the RV life is all about. You'll soon see the good and bad things about the lifestyle, as well as learning about the different types of RVs and their pluses and minuses.

For those of you who like hardcopy books, the "Trailer Life Campground Directory" has been popular with RVers for many years.

Some Benefits of the RV Life

The RV life has many benefits, things RVers will extol when they tell you about how great their life is. These include a variety of places to go and things to see. One doesn't ever have to get bored when RVng—all you have to do if some place isn't interesting enough is move to a new place—problem solved. And you can move every day if you want, assuming you can afford the gas—or conversely, stay put if you're in a good place.

Another benefit of the RV life is freedom. This isn't just the freedom to come and go as you please, but is also the freedom to make your own rules—within reason, of course. You get up when you want, go to bed when you want, eat when you want, etc. Of course, most retirees can do this, but the difference is, if you have an irritating neighbor, you can leave them behind.

If you get in a difficult situation, such as a place with too many rules, you can just leave. If you see that a bad storm is coming in tomorrow, you can choose to try and outrun it or you can stay. Too windy? Not a problem, head somewhere else. Too hot? Ditto.

Like our nomadic ancestors, you can choose to follow the sun, heading south for the winter and north for the summer. You're in charge of your own happiness, and you're free to change whatever is making you unhappy.

Another benefit of RVing is having your own bed wherever you go. You basically take your house with you, like a turtle, but with better accommodations. No more motels and wondering who was there before you and if the place really got properly cleaned. No being awakened in the middle of the night because the walls are too thin. No being forced to eat out all the time when traveling—you can enjoy exactly what you like to eat, no matter where you are, because you have it stocked in your cupboards and refrigerator. You can turn the heat up or down when you want and have your pets with you. And while some parts of the U.S. experience a bedbug epidemic, it's mostly irrelevant to you.

When you decide to go visit family or friends, your time is of a higher quality because you're not depending on them for your accommodations. You can go to bed when you want and get up without worrying about waking your hosts. Instead of being guests, you're temporary neighbors, and you don't have to worry as much about overstaying your welcome.

The RV life is generally more cost effective than living in a regular house, although this does depend on how much you choose to travel and where you stay. If you boondock, your cost of living becomes very minimal, basically being no more than your food and necessities and a bit of gas. And because your home is so small, you tend to be very careful about recreational shopping. You don't want any more stuff, so you won't spend your money frivolously.

One of the best things about RVing is meeting like-minded people, and many of them can tell amazing stories. They'll introduce you to new ways to cook things, new ways to do things, and new places to go.

The network of full-time RVers is amazing, and everyone can tell stories of serendipitous meetings, as nomadic paths seem to cross often. You'll be out in the middle of the Arizona desert and have someone you met in Washington come over and invite you to dinner. Some of the stories I've heard about paths crossing are truly incredible.

And there's something about hanging around with like-minded souls that affirms that what you're doing is the right thing. You can satisfy your wanderlust while staying in your own home—and that home is easy to clean compared to a sticks and bricks.

One of the best things about the RV life is that your world becomes bigger. Once you see what's out there, you tend to become truly amazed at the diversity of people and cultures, even if you never leave the United States. And the landscapes you'll travel through will stay with you forever in your photos and memories.

Some Drawbacks of the RV Life

Of course, everything has its drawbacks, and RVing is no exception. But being aware of these beforehand can mitigate the impacts and help you plan for them.

One of the first things people notice when they start RVing is how small of a space they now have to live in. It doesn't seem to matter how big your rig is, it seems your stuff will expand to fill it and you'll still feel crowded.

There's a popular cartoon on the internet that shows a couple in a small trailer, crammed full of stuff. The next few panels show that same couple in bigger and bigger RVs, each crammed with more and more stuff, until the final cartoon shows them in a big Class A, all crammed with stuff.

RVers tend to create outdoor spaces to extend their living area. They'll buy screen tents and large outdoor rugs and patio furniture, as well as barbecues and solar patio lights and that sort of thing.

You need a place to store all this when you're on the road, so those with smaller rigs are more frugal, even though the smaller the rig, the more time you'll want to spend outside. Even inclement weather won't stop some, as they set up all kinds of things that extend their rigs.

Some of the more elaborate patios are those of the folks with big rigs, as they have space to store it all, but even a tiny teardrop trailer can double or triple its size with some creative screen tents and a couple of camp chairs. You quickly learn to become very efficient at storing things and putting them away when space is at a minimum.

Another thing many have problems with is the feeling of loss of community. This tends to seem to bother the sociable types more than the loners, as the sociable types usually leave behind a large network of friends and family. But just because you're no longer in their vicinity doesn't mean you can't stay in touch and return to visit.

Opportunities to meet new friends on the road are totally dependent on your own desires to do so. You can boondock alone out in the wilds and never meet anyone, or you can hang out in places like the Slabs (Slab City in California) or Quartzite (Arizona) and quickly meet more people than imaginable. The main problem with such new friendships is that your friends are, like you, nomads, so they soon move on.

Some join clubs and such, which make your odds of reconnecting much greater, as you can attend the club's organized functions. Some clubs are based on the type of rig you own, such as the Casita Club or the T@b Club (the T@b is a cute teardrop-shaped trailer with a loyal following).

In my experience, the fiberglass rig owners (such as Casitas, Scamps, UHauls, Bolers, Burros, Escapes, Egg-campers, etc.) tend to stick together more than those who own other types of rigs. Maybe it's from having a certain outlook on life, as they also tend to be more frugal and self-sufficient.

Other clubs are based on being single, and these are often also ways to meet potential mates, if you're in the field for that. And clubs like Sisters on the Fly share common interests (in this case, glamping and flyfishing—glamping is a term for camping in vintage trailers decorated to the nines). Other large clubs like the Escapees provide a means to meet like-minded RVers, as well as providing many other amenities, such as long-term RV parks.

Another thing some have problems with is never knowing where community amenities are and always feeling like you're kind of lost. You want a really good steak dinner, but you have no idea which place in your current locale qualifies. This lack of continuity can get really disconcerting, but it often is resolved the longer you travel, as you return to places that are now familiar.

It's always a bit unsettling to pull into a place and have no idea where to camp, get groceries, or do laundry. There are a number of books out that attempt to fill this gap (such as the Escapee Club's "Day's End," a directory with information about communities), but perhaps the best way is to just ask around. Most locals are happy to help. And, as I mentioned before, another good way to deal with this is to follow the many good blogs on the internet that fellow RVers have.

If you're not traveling solo, you may find it's difficult to adjust to living in a small space with someone else, even if they're your spouse. You must both be comfortable in small spaces, as well as comfortable with each other, or you may have difficulties. Of course, when the weather's nice, you can go outside, but when you're stuck inside for days on end because of bad weather, underlying tensions are sure to come out.

One of the harder things about living in a small space is the necessity of always moving stuff. Your outside gear often has to be moved in and out depending on the weather, especially if it's windy. Vehicles are good for this, for example, I carry my portable solar panel in my truck, along with my camp chair and table. It's helpful to have a pickup with a topper or some sort of van to store things in.

Having a small space often necessitates a lot of activity. For example, I cook and make coffee outside on my little one-burner stove, using the inside stove as counter space. I'm always going in and out, up and down, and tasks that are simple in a house become much more work, and it seems you're always going back and forth.

This keeps you in shape, but if you're an impatient person, be forewarned that sometimes all you'll feel like you do is housekeeping chores, which of course is far from true. It's ironic, as your house may be as small as 60 square feet.

The key to happy and simple RVing is to be flexible and adaptable. Conditions will vary every day, but usually they all tend to fall within a certain spectrum, and the more you do it, the more of an old-hand you become at it.

How to Get Started

This is probably the toughest part of the entire full-timing equation—how to extract yourself from the morass of daily life and become a full-timer.

First, it helps to have money, but even then, it can be a long and difficult task getting from the sticks and bricks lifestyle to that of the RV life.

But what if you don't have the money you need to get started? That's a tough one, but it's a problem that can be solved, given that you're willing to compromise. You may not live in the style you want, but if you really want to get out there, you can do it on a pretty tight budget.

It may seem like an impossible task, but the first thing you need to do is decide how committed you are to doing this, as it may not be easy. If you're simply wanting to escape your current life, maybe you should first examine if there aren't options that might be more suitable.

For example, if you hate your boss, maybe finding another job is a better solution than chucking everything and living on the road. Full-timing is not necessarily an easy life, as it has its own problems and challenges. Be sure you're trading one set of problems for a set that's better, not a set that's even more difficult.

OK, you're absolutely sure you want to full-time. You're not just looking for an easy escape from your current problems, you really want to live in an RV. How does one proceed?

First, take stock of your responsibilities. You may want to run away from them, but that's not how to do things. You have to determine which responsibilities are dispensable and which aren't.

For example, it goes without debate that you take your pets with you or you don't go. Same with any other responsibilities where you're a caretaker. These are not things you can just up and leave, unless you can find others who will help you out. But don't underestimate your abilities to make difficult situations work. One full-timer pulls a horse trailer that has living quarters in it—and her horses! She also has dogs and a goat. They're a well-travelled bunch and seem quite content.

Often we end up with responsibilities that are self-created. This involves things like debts and relationships that aren't necessarily good for us. Such things are pretty much self-explanatory, like the so-called friend who always comes over on weekends to do their laundry and raid your refrigerator.

If you're deep in debt (and most Americans are), you have to start working your way out. This will take sacrifices, but they'll be forgotten, believe me, once the debt is gone. You'll forget about all those lattes you had to forego to pay off that extra $150 per month on your credit card bill.

But sometimes your debts can't be paid in your lifetime, or at least it seems that way. You may owe another 25 years on your mortgage. And if you're like many, you owe more on your house than what it's worth, so selling it isn't really even an option. What to do? Getting out seems like an impossible task. It feels like you're stuck in the La Brea Tar Pits and sinking fast.

There's always a solution to a problem, but sometimes it may not be one you like. You may have to rent your house out rather than selling it. Or maybe you should see if the bank will let you sell it at a loss (a short sale, but be advised that the IRS may tax you on the perceived gains, so always talk with someone who knows the ins and outs of such).

One solution may be to declare bankruptcy or to even just walk away, but once again, educate yourself on the possible ramifications. Many people find this akin to stealing from the banks, but it's simply a contract where if you don't keep your end, they get your house back.

If you're renting, things will be easier for you, as you can dissolve that agreement with adequate notice. You can sell everything you own to buy an RV, even if it's just an old van.

Once you have your RV, you can apply the money you used for renting to your living expenses. We'll talk more about where that money can potentially come from later, but all in all, you may have to scrape and barely get by until you've saved enough for a rig and can get away. But as they say, where there's a will, there's a way, and it's true in this case.

Getting Free of Stuff

The old saying that "you don't own stuff, it owns you" is definitely true. If you're going to live in a small space, you won't have room for most of your stuff. The first step in getting ready for full-timing is getting rid of absolutely everything you won't need, and that's probably about 95 percent or more of what you own. The good side to this is you can sometimes sell your stuff and make enough money to help finance an RV.

This is often the hardest part of the whole full-timing process, as it involves discarding not only the things you've spent your life accumulating, but also discarding the mindset we're taught from birth, that stuff is good and a measure of our self-worth—the "he who dies with the most stuff wins" mindset. It seems like the consumer mindset we're taught from birth goes hand-in-hand with the idea that it's OK to be in debt, that you owe it to yourself to have all these nice things. It's another part of the Great American Dream.

Well, what you really owe to yourself is to live how you want, to wake up each morning to an entire day full of hours and minutes that you can do with exactly what you wish, not working hard to pay off some banker's new house.

Getting rid of everything can be very difficult for most people, especially if you're older and have spent most of your life accumulating nice things for your house. It can be painful to part with these things, as they can represent a part of your life, as well as reminding you of places and people. I've seen grown adults cry at yard sales—some with happiness because the stuff is going away, and some with sadness for the same reason.

Even if you're not sure how you're going to accomplish this new RV life you want to live, it's a good idea to start with getting rid of your stuff. Start with the things that you haven't used for some time, those things stored in your basement or guest-room closets.

You have to be brutal or the stuff will stay—just keep reminding yourself that someday your kids will thank you because they won't have to go through all your junk when you die. In fact, kids can be a good place to get rid of stuff. They're often happy to get the things you took so long to acquire. Or maybe your kids are more savvy than that, or maybe you don't have kids. If so, there are always places like the Goodwill and Habitat for Humanity, who will often drive to your door and collect the stuff, saving you having to cart it away.

Please take my advice and don't put your things into storage unless you think you may want to abandon the RV life someday. Storage units will generally end up costing you more than it would cost to replace the stuff, unless you have some really nice and unique things.

I personally (with help) moved enough stuff to furnish a 2,000-square foot house to several large storage units, thinking I would someday use it again. After storing it for several years and realizing I would probably never again own a house, I eventually ended up giving most of it away, which is what I should've done from the start. Storage is a very expensive option, and most things can be replaced. The money you spend on storage can be hard to replace.

Be prepared for your family and friends to not understand why you're doing this, and in some cases, to actively try to discourage you. Those who don't understand won't ever understand, no matter how you try to explain. Your family may even resort to tactics of guilt and fear to dissuade you—what if you get sick out there all alone, or how can you just leave us here like this? This often comes from those who didn't pay you much mind at all until you decided to follow your own path.

Or—and this may be even harder—be prepared for those you thought would care about what you're doing to act like they don't. They won't miss you and may not even come to your aid when you need help moving that huge solid oak entertainment center. Their indifference can be brutally painful, but in the long run, we each have to live our own lives.

If people try to tell you you're being irresponsible, it may be important for you to continually remind yourself that you need to do this to be a responsible person, as you're responsible for your own health and happiness, and living a life you don't enjoy will eventually kill you.

Finally, there's something about paring down your things to the necessities that gives you a feeling of being in control, even if it seems you're really no closer to any concrete goals than before. You're beginning the lightening up process which is so necessary to successful RV living.

We really don't need much to live happy and fulfilling lives—what we need is our freedom. Like my mom always said about stuff, "They won't let you take a moving van with you when you die."

Organization

Getting rid of stuff goes hand in hand with being organized. I'm not normally a very organized person, and believe it or not, having to be organized can be very frustrating for me (I hate having to put things away right after I use them), but when you're living in a small space it becomes a necessity.

The smaller the rig, the more organized you need to be. You will be forced to really pare down your stuff. You may think you're a minimalist, but you'll be surprised at how much stuff you actually don't need when you move into an RV.

You'll decide you don't need two coffee cups, and one will go to the Goodwill—and this after you thought you got rid of everything you wouldn't use. A lot of beginning RVers leave a trail of stuff behind them for their first few months on the road (no, hopefully not at camp sites).

You get to where you don't want gifts and tell family not to buy you anything, but buying stuff is part of our culture and it's hard to make them understand. Sometimes it's just better to accept things and then re-gift them to a new home.

People who don't live in RVs don't understand the constraints. Not only do you not have room, but you don't want to deal with the constant packing and repacking of things to get to other things you do want and need.

When you live in a small space, you often have to stack things or put it in rows, with less-used stuff at the back. Then when you need it, you have to move everything. Your life becomes a zen exercise in moving and repacking things.

If you're like me, basically disorganized, this becomes one of the hardest things about the RV life, and also probably the number one reason people ditch the smaller rigs for something with more space.

But it's a trade-off, as you now have your big 30-foot fifth wheeler and lots of room (which will quickly fill up), but you still have to tow it all, and that means more gas and being more careful where you go. You'll also have fewer boondocking places, as you can no longer just take off on some little dirt road to see what's there, because you may not be able to turn around.

And if you do decide you want all that stuff and get a bigger rig, your number one concern may become gas mileage. Be prepared to replace your lack of space with a lack of dollars in your pocket. Whoops, we can't go anywhere for two weeks until that check's deposited, but we don't really want to anyway because it's a hassle hauling that big rig around. Some people don't mind this, as they stay in a park and move around less.

So, being organized can have far-reaching implications. But one thing you have with most RVing is the satisfaction of knowing that everything you own in that little trailer following along behind you can all be replaced if anything happens, unless you're carrying priceless family photos, which probably isn't wise (digitize and store them). If you're a minimalist and haven't spent much, even the trailer can be easily replaced.

Swap that little trailer for a big fifth wheel or Class A? It might be tempting if you have the money—lots of room, luxury, appliances, etc., but now you need power to run it all and that usually mean hookups or a generator, which means hauling gas.

RVing is all about tradeoffs of one kind or another.

Getting a Rig

You're in the process of getting rid of everything—all those unnecessary things that are holding you back. You may not own a house, which will make things easier, but if you do, hopefully you're getting it ready to put on the market or rent, unless you can afford to keep it as a home base.

You probably now have a very uncertain feeling, one of what to do once this all comes together. Hopefully, you can afford to now start looking to purchase a rig, which will ease those fears. But if you can't buy anything until your house sells, you can still be prepared for that day and then act quickly.

This is when the internet is your friend, for you can do most of the research you need online. And odds are good you've already done this and have a feel for what you want. In that case, it's now a good time to start actually visiting dealers and looking at rigs first-hand.

Some don't have the luxury of cashing out a house to buy a rig, and in these economic times, many homeowners actually will walk away owing more than they got for their house. If this is you, how can you afford to buy a rig at all?

Some may spend all their money on rent and the necessities of life and can't manage to save anything. It's a vicious cycle—you can't afford a rig because you have to pay your house payment or rent each month. If you had a rig, you could instead use that money to make a payment on it, eventually freeing yourself from the hopelessness.

If you can get a bank loan, this is one of the few times it may be a prudent thing to do. If you can finance an RV and thereby leave the rent behind, instead applying that money to your RV, then you're in a good situation, as long as you don't get into more than you can handle financially.

But buying an expensive RV on a 20-year plan is just a new form of shackles, so don't do it. Instead, buy the best rig you can get for the least money. Your goal is to get it paid off so your freedom becomes more obtainable. If you have an RV payment, you have to generate that much income each month on top of your living expenses.

It's easy to justify getting something for as much as the bank will loan you, saying you'll get a nice RV and never need to buy another or some such logic. But that RV may end up keeping you in bondage for a long time, and it also may not be the best rig for you after all. You may decide you need something bigger or smaller or narrower or wider.

If there's any way you can get a rig without involving a bank, then that's always the best choice. Maybe you have a good friend who will loan you some cash at a reasonable interest rate. Or maybe it's time to cash in those stocks and bonds your parents left you. Or best yet, maybe you have something you can sell, lightening your load while generating money for an RV at the same time.

You may have to be creative, and you may not get anything close to what you want, but the goal is to get a rig. Not having any debt allows you to save your money to do other things, which always means more freedom, even if those other things may include someday getting a new rig.

It's best to pay cash if you can, as you thereby avoid interest and also have the option of whether or not to insure. If you own your rig with the bank, they get to determine what kind of insurance you need, and it can be more costly. I would recommend at the very least getting roadside assistance, but if you own your rig, you get to determine how much insurance you want, not the bank.

Once you find a rig that works for you, it's best to stop looking at that point. That way you're not tempted to want something you probably can't afford.

So, what kind of rig should you get? Well, that answer depends entirely on you and your likes and dislikes, but it's a very important decision that shouldn't be taken lightly. There are as many types of rigs as there are choices in housing, and it's almost impossible to list them all. Other RV books go into this in great detail, but really, the main choice is this: do you want to tow it or ride in it?

Ride in It

If you want to ride in it, then your main choices are a Class A, a Class C, or a Class B. These are all motorized vehicles that carry the RV. Some of these are very luxurious and are as close to having a house on wheels as you can get.

The Class A is like a bus (with a flat front), allowing the driver to perch up high and look down on the world. These are mounted on a large truck chassis and are the largest option you'll have for a motorhome. They are difficult to drive until you get used to them, but they also provide some safety in that you're up above cars and their spray when the roads are wet, and you can see further ahead.

Class A's that have big diesel engines in the rear are called diesel pushers and tend to be much more expensive to buy and maintain than their non-diesel counterparts, yet they tend to last longer. You may find a Class A for a good price, but keep in mind that an oil change may cost several hundreds of dollars, and don't forget the size and number of tires on those rigs.

There's a reason people who own these big rigs tend to not fit my idea of the simple RV life—they're expensive and you pretty much have to drive them on good roads and stay in campgrounds. Repairs can be astronomical, not to mention gas mileage—think five m.p.g. for some of these behemoths. Don't let their luxurious interiors fool you—there's a world of maintenance in there and they also tend to depreciate fairly fast.

The Class C is smaller and generally less expensive than the Class A, but can also come in as costing a bundle. They also depreciate quickly, though they tend to get better mileage, depending on their length and weight, as they're smaller. Class C's are mounted on a chassis with a bunk area usually located above the driver. They're easier to drive and to maneuver into small camp sites. Many Class C's are just as luxurious as their Class A counterparts.

Class B's are luxury vans and can cost almost as much as a Class A or C. They tend to get better mileage as they weigh less, and are easier to drive and handle, usually fitting in the same parking spot as a car. They typically have very nice interiors that are complete with beds, kitchens, and bathrooms.

Not all vans start as Class B's, as some are regular vans that have been converted into RVs. Conversion vans are popular in urban areas where people want to stealth camp. Some conversion vans, like the Mercedes Sprinter, can be quite expensive. These are often owner conversions and some are quite nice.

Also in the owner-conversion category is the converted bus, which can be anything from a small school bus (the "skoolie") on up to a Greyhound-type rig. These are pretty easy to find on places like Craigslist, as their owners get tired of working on them, trying to find a place to park them, and having to take out a bank loan to pay for gas to drive them. But some people truly love them.

Many big rig owners tow a smaller vehicle behind their rig, which is called a "toad" (towed). This is so they can get around once they park the rig—go sightseeing, get groceries, etc.

Types of toads are as variable as RVs—just remember that you can't back up your rig while pulling a toad. Also, once you have a toad, you now have two vehicles with engines and tires and all to maintain.

Tow It

If you prefer towing your home instead of driving it, your first acquisition, unless you already have one, will be a tow vehicle. Obviously, if you pull a trailer, you only have one engine to maintain, which is a plus in my simplicity book.

Be sure your tow vehicle is suited to pulling the trailer you get, which means you have to understand how much weight you can pull. Unless you're pulling a very light trailer, you'll want a transmission cooler in your tow vehicle, if you don't want your transmission to go out.

There are, once again, a variety of types of trailers, and I'll include pickup campers here, though they're actually a world of their own. But a lot of the same rules apply with campers as with trailers—your rig has to be able to carry or pull it.

In general, besides campers, which fit in the bed of your truck, the varieties of trailers include travel trailers, fifth wheels, hybrids (hard-sided trailers with pop-out ends and/or sides that are canvas), and pop-ups (both soft sided and hard sided). These kinds of rigs are also called towables, with the exception of pickup campers.

If you've ever gone to an RV show (and you should), you'll quickly realize how many different types of towables are out there—it's almost overwhelming trying to decide what you want and need.

The best place to start, if you're new to all this, is with something small. That way you don't have a fortune invested, and you can also quickly find out if you're up to towing. Some people hate towing, and some actually enjoy the process of hooking up and hitting the road. In fact, there's a term for it, "hitch-itch," which applies to the desire to get hooked up and going.

Fifth-wheel trailers (often called "fivers") are often the opposite of small, although you can find some in the smaller range. Most fifth wheelers must be towed by heavy-duty trucks, and their mount point is in the truck bed, allowing for very large tow weights.

These trailers can rival the big Class A's and C's for amenities, and are often fitted with slide-outs (also called tip-outs), as are many of the Class A's and C's and even a few B's. Slide-outs make your rig bigger by allowing you to expand part of one (or more) walls after you're setup. Note that slide-outs can be death for cats, so if you get one and have animals, confine them before moving the slide-out in or out.

Slide-outs can get stuck, and I've heard more than a few horror stories about people being stuck in place and unable to move their rig because they can't get their slide-out closed. Not even a tow-truck works in such scenarios, and getting an RV repairman to your site might be a costly or even impossible venture.

If you're used to pulling a big rig, a fifth wheel can be a good solution for those wanting a rig with a more permanent home feel with lots of space. But be aware that pulling them and getting them into camping spots can be an exercise not for the light of heart. They're also difficult to boondock with, as are most big rigs.

If you're on a limited budget (and who isn't?), it might be best to spend a lot of time looking before deciding what you want. But a rule of thumb among RVers is that you'll end up with multiple rigs before finding what suits you best. It just seems inevitable.

I myself have had two popup pickup campers, a big hardside pickup camper (a Lance), three 17-foot Casitas (fiberglass trailers), a 13-foot Burro (another fiberglass trailer), and my current rig, an 18-foot Aliner (a hardside popup trailer). In addition, I've tent camped for many years, camped in my pickup shell, and lived for a short time in a friend's small Class C, as well as staying in my uncle's fifth-wheel trailer and my family's vintage trailer.

Keep in mind that, just like the car industry, the RV industry has a vested interest in getting you to trade up. There are always new designs with new bells and whistles to catch your eye.

A truism among RV wheeling and dealing is that your rig will probably depreciate, no matter how well you take care of it. RVs are just like cars in that respect, with a few exceptions: fiberglass trailers, Airstreams, and some vintage models. All three of these types tend to hold their values better than regular trailers.

Many trailers have fiberglass skins, but true fiberglass trailers are built like boats—using fiberglass molds, with fiberglass making up the entire body, not just the skin. They are often touted as being more durable than non-fiberglass trailers, as they're not subject to delamination and leaking.

Types of fiberglass trailers include the very popular Casita, its cousin the Scamp, and various other brands, such as the Burro, U-Haul, and Boler, the latter three which are no longer being manufactured.

Canada seems to have gotten in the fiberglass act in a spectacular way with the Bigfoot and the Escape, both which have good reputations for their quality and insulating values.

Many of the fiberglass trailers are easy to tow, as they weigh less than a regular trailer and are typically narrower, with the exception of the Bigfoot. Their rounded corners, however, which are from being molded, are a detriment in some people's minds, as they result in a smaller interior with compromised space.

Some trailers, like the Casita and Scamp, use ensolite interiors (a furry carpet-like covering, fondly called "rat fur"). The combination of the rounded shape, furry walls, and small windows give these trailers a closed-in feeling, which some find cozy and others find claustrophobic.

I finally gave up on fiberglass trailers, as I find them too confining. However, the fiberglass people are a loyal group and really love their little fiberglass "eggs," and the units are typically very well built. In fact, saying it's a loyal group is probably an understatement—almost a cult might be closer to the truth, especially with the Casita owners.

There are a number of forums dedicated to the fiberglass eggs. On a side note, the eggs are not prone to hail damage, as are most other types of rigs, and I will say that most fiberglass owners also belong to the simplicity and common-sense clubs that I greatly admire.

If you like the fiberglass eggs, they're always easy to sell, and often at a profit. I would recommend one as a place to start, since they are so easy to sell, and you can't go wrong if it's not to your liking. But if you find one you like, jump on it, as they often sell within hours of posting.

Be sure to get the rig that matches your lifestyle. If you like to boondock, make sure you have lots of clearance. If you have a lot of pets, you might want a bigger rig so you're not tripping over them all the time. Or if you have a hobby, you may want extra space to accommodate that.

In any case, getting the right rig may take awhile, but it's an important decision, so be sure what you get will work for you.

Picking a Home Base

Some full-time RVers choose to register their rigs in states with no taxes (such as South Dakota, Texas, and Montana) and thus save money, but you have to also become residents of such states, which usually requires at least one trip to obtain a driver's license. There are businesses that will serve as mailboxes for you and generally facilitate your residency rules, but they do charge monthly fees.

But if you're not a full-timer and do have a house and try to register your vehicle in another state, be careful, as some states are going after such violators in earnest, Colorado being one. Always be sure you're above board on everything you do in such regards.

If you are a full-timer, your home base is called your RV domicile, and where you choose to be registered is a very important decision. You have to call one state home, even if you never stay there. Your RV domicile is where you get your mail and pay your taxes, as well as register your vehicles and get your driver's license. Your domicile isn't actually the same as a residence (your rig is your residence), it's just the state you choose to "belong to."

If you have your driver's license from one state, your vehicles registered in another, and maybe get your mail in yet another, you are probably breaking the law in all three states and may be subject to fines. And if they all decide to come after you for state taxes, you'll be hard pressed to prove you're not a resident of any of the three. That's why it's important to pick one state and stick with it.

If you still own a home that you occupy even part time, the state it's in will probably be considered your domicile. But if you don't own a home, you're free to pick whichever state you want. Be aware, though, that the state your Social Security check is deposited in can also be considered your domicile based on that fact alone.

Various states have various benefits associated with choosing them as a domicile, and it's best to become familiar with them before choosing.

Once you decide which state you want, you need to get an address there. Sometimes you can do this via a UPS or Mailboxes store. You then need to transfer all your registrations to that state. RV mail-forwarding services will help you do this, as well as forward your mail to you from your new address, which they will even provide.

Full-timers typically plan ahead enough that they can get their mail forwarded to a General Delivery box in some town down the road ahead.

The more popular states for full-timers include Alaska, Florida, Nevada, South Dakota, Texas, Washington, and Wyoming. That's because these states have no state income tax. South Dakota is especially popular because it's friendly to RVers wishing to become residents and has various RV mail forwarding services.

Some states don't have any sales tax, so RVers will choose them for residency, especially when buying a big expensive rig. These states include: Alaska, Delaware, Montana, New Hampshire, and Oregon. Note the distinction here between sales tax and income tax.

When choosing a state, be sure you know whether or not that state requires you to show up in person to renew your driver's license. Your auto and RV insurance may also vary in cost by state.

Life on the Road

The most important thing an RVer can have is a positive attitude. This can be more important than your rig, as I've met people full-timing in tents who were quite happy. In fact, the campground I host at part-time has had hosts who had nothing but tents. A good positive attitude will get you much farther than anything with wheels.

It seems like it's human nature to want more than we have, and envy can destroy about any picnic. I've seen it over and over—people with perfectly good rigs who were pretty happy until they saw something bigger and nicer, then they let themselves start thinking about how great it would be to have that, and soon it's a downward spiral.

I think it's perfectly fine to aspire to better things, but it's your attitude about it that counts. If you want a better rig, that's fine, just don't let it spoil your happiness. Enjoy what you have to the fullest.

I myself have been the victim of my own wishes more than once. When I lived in a house, I thought nothing of it, and I would see nicer homes and want something better. But after living in a tent for months at a time (with dogs and cats), when I rented a house again, I wasn't quite so picky about what I had.

I enjoyed the running water, indoor plumbing, big comfy bed (even though it really wasn't big nor very comfy), and shelter from the elements. I love the RV life most of the time, but when I do stay in a house, I fully appreciate the comforts.

And so, how much you enjoy your life on the road is pretty much determined by you. Sure, things will happen to make you unhappy, but these things happen when you're living in a house, also. That's just life, and how you deal with it determines how happy you are.

If you head out with realistic expectations, you'll find that sometimes life throws you a curve ball, and other times it brings you roses. You may wake to find you have a flat tire, then minutes later witness the most amazing sunrise ever.

It seems that the RV life has the potential for more ups and downs, and it definitely has less potential for boredom. Even if you stay in the same spot for some time, you'll seldom be bored, as you're closer to the natural world, and it's also much more difficult to get stuck in a rut when you move around.

So, what's a typical day like for an RVer? I actually don't think there is such a thing as a typical day. Every day is what you make of it. That may sound cliche, but it's true, especially in the RV world.

For example, you may decide to just lollygag around all day and read a book or play your guitar or fiddle with your ham radio or play with the dogs. Or, you may decide to go sightseeing and explore the countryside around you. Another day may be errands day when you get groceries and do laundry. Or, you may decide to go for a bike ride or play golf.

This may start to sound like an endless vacation, but it's a life that you get to design. If you like keeping busy, you may decide to go volunteer at the local animal shelter or the local library. Or maybe you have a hobby you enjoy, like silversmithing. I know one RVer who makes stunning quilts and sells them while on the road, financing her travels.

In short, the RV life is what you make of it. If you're the kind of person who needs supervision, you probably won't have any, unless you travel with a partner who will tell you what to do. RVers are typically self-motivated independent types who figure things out as they go.

But really, what's a typical day like for an RVer? Well, it's impossible to say, as everyone's different, but I can tell you what a typical day is not like:

- You won't be mowing the lawn, trimming the hedges, killing weeds, or tending your garden (though some RVers do have small container gardens they take with them).
- You won't be fixing plumbing (unless it's on your RV), painting the house, or cleaning out the basement.
- You won't be repairing the shingles that blew off in the last windstorm.
- You won't be playing pool in your rec room (though you might be playing pool in the RV park's rec room), and you won't be luxuriating in your big massage chair (unless you own a big rig).
- You won't be worrying about making your mortgage payment.
- You won't be cussing out your neighbors for having

a noisy party all hours of the night (it can still happen, but now you can just move).

- You won't be shampooing carpets.
- You won't be wishing for the millionth time that the neighbor's dog would quit barking (it can still happen, but again, you can move).
- You won't be wondering how you're going to pay this year's property taxes after the city just raised them.
- You won't be worrying that your community's crime rate just went up.

The list of things you won't be doing is almost endless. Here are a few of the things you might be doing:

- You might be worrying about where your next camp will be. This will involve getting out your maps and daydreaming about where to go next, except it's not really a daydream, it's something you can actually do.
- You might be looking for a place to dump your gray and black water tanks.
- You might be kayaking on that lake you're camped by.
- You might be dealing with a blown out tire or a blown out fuse.
- You might be watching a beautiful golden eagle soaring above.
- You might be dealing with an inoperative fridge with no repairman nearby.
- You might be worrying that a big storm is coming in and hoping it's not too windy. This will be accompanied by taking your awning or shade shelter down.

- You might be out hiking a trail that starts right at your door.
- You might be cooking a gourmet dinner on your outside grill and wondering which bottle of wine would go best with it.
- You might be wishing you had decent internet reception.
- You might be leaving a place you don't like—without even having to give notice.
- You might be wishing it weren't time to do that pesky laundry again because the nearest laundromat is a dump.
- You might be looking for a good place to get water, driving around town with your water jugs.
- You might be thinking about moving because of that shady-looking character that camped nearby.
- Or, better, you might be over talking to your new neighbor, who just happens to love ham radio, just like you do.
- You might be watching an incredible sunrise or sunset.

And on and on, both bad and good.

My mom used to tell me that when one moved, you just traded one set of problems for another. She wasn't a pessimist, just a realist, and it is true. When you adopt the full-time RV life, you still have problems, they're just different from those of the sticks and bricks life.

So, if you're thinking your life in an RV will be carefree, it's simply not true. No life on Planet Earth is carefree, and studies have shown we do better and are actually even happier when we have challenges. The degree and type of challenge can make all the difference, though, and it seems to me that RVing has more interesting challenges than most lifestyles.

My mom also said that one could never really know where they wanted to live without first trying a place out. With RVing, one gets to try out lots of different places, and if you do decide to settle down, odds are much better you'll end up in a place you really want to be.

Is RVing Physically Difficult?

RVing can be physically difficult, depending on the type of rig you have, where you camp, and if you're alone or not. If you have a pop-up camper, for example, and have a bad back, well, the two just typically don't go together.

No matter what kind of rig you have, there will always be some physical aspects to keeping things going. Unlike with a house, where you can hire out your cleaning and yard work, living in an RV requires certain tasks that you just simply have to do yourself.

For example, hooking and unhooking your rig may take a certain amount of labor, depending on the rig. I've watched people jumping up and down on their hitches and pushing the tongues of their rigs back and forth, all in an attempt to get things properly aligned. But if your rig is hard to hitch up, you can always get a new hitch installed, or even an electric hitch, making it a simple task.

As mentioned earlier, popups can be hard to deal with, and someone who isn't physically fit might want to avoid them. However, many popups are now fitted with electric lifts, making them easy to put up and down.

Many older or less fit people opt for the Class A's, B's, and C's because they are easier to deal with. All your stuff is right there in your rig and you never have to hitch or unhitch. Of course, this simplicity is negated for some by having a toad and also by having to deal with fewer available sites, especially if you have a really big rig.

No matter what you have, there's always the chore of setting up your outside stuff—your chairs, outdoor rug, barbecue, shade shelter, or whatever you may have. These items can be heavy and hard to handle. If you're elderly or have problems carrying stuff, you can always find a work around, though it may simply be not setting up as much stuff.

Other chores will require some effort, the amount again depending on the type of rig you have and where you camp. If you stay in campgrounds or RV parks with hookups, you won't have to worry about getting water or dealing with your trash.

If you boondock, your life will be more physically difficult, as you'll be hauling trash and water and driving more to deal with such things. In addition, some have portable solar panels, which can be heavy, which you won't need if you have hookups.

I have personally stayed in a park with hookups only once in my life, and that was at Valley of Gods in Nevada (the campground where I host has dry camping only). I had just bought a Casita down in Arizona and was on my way home. It was cold and the Casita had no heater, just a heat strip on the AC, which meant I needed electrical hookups to stay warm. I stopped the next day and bought a Little Buddy portable propane heater, which I used after that.

As a lifelong boondocker, I've had my share of hard labor, especially when it comes to hauling water. Since the campground I host in doesn't provide water, rather than take my trailer into town every time I need water and fill the tanks, I just haul water in seven-gallon jugs. These are heavy (a gallon of water weighs 8.35 pounds), so I have a table I can scoot them onto from the back of my pickup, rather than lifting them.

This is just one example of a workaround you can use if you have physical limitations, and many RVers do, especially since full-timers tend to be older folks (younger people often don't have the resources to RV, which is often simply a Social Security check). Like I mentioned earlier, if you're not camping alone, things get easier.

One thing about RVing, it tends to help get you into shape and keep you there. Not too long ago, I fractured two vertebrae and was pretty much incapable of doing anything for nine months, which in itself was pure torture, not to mention the accompanying pain. After awhile, I was determined to start doing more, and I knew getting back in my trailer would help get me back into shape.

At first, I could barely climb the steps into my little Casita, and doing anything was really difficult. Keep in mind I was dry camping (no hookups) and also had cats and dogs in my care. Every day seemed like the last I'd be able to camp, yet every day I got a little stronger.

Some days I would sit and want to cry because of the pain and difficulty of doing anything, but by the end of three months I was remarkably better and doing things I'd considered impossible when I first started. I figured out ways to make things easier.

I've read of folks in their 80's that full-time RV, and I've also seen people in wheelchairs living on their own in RVs which have been modified for them. I've also read and heard many stories of people with immune system problems that were remarkably better once they got into the RV lifestyle. A close friend's depression seems to abate when he's RVing.

The upshot of all this is, yes, RVing can be difficult, but it doesn't have to be. If you have issues that hold you back physically, you just have to be sure to get the best kind of rig for alleviating those problems and be able to stay in places that make your life easier. This will probably mean you need more money, but not necessarily.

My experience has been that many handicapped people make up for their handicaps with their attitudes and can enjoy the RV life as much as anyone, with some careful planning. The same goes for anyone who is constrained because of their age.

One of the best things about the RV life is that you'll meet many folks on the road who are good-hearted and more than happy to help you out when you need it.

Getting Sick or Injured

A few years ago, I'd just bought a little 13-foot fiberglass Burro and was anxious to get back into the RV life after a winter hiatus renting a house. I hardly expected what was to come.

I thought I was prepared, but I wasn't prepared for getting sick. I had four dogs and two cats to care for, and though the dogs were old hands at camping, the cats had never camped. They were uncertain and insecure about it.

I'd taken Spice-Cat for a number of hikes on his little halter, so he wasn't completely new to it all, but Mindy-Cat was, even though she'd been living outside on her own when I rescued her.

To make a long story short, I ended up really sick on the road. I ended up with a bronchial infection that I thought was over when I started camping, but it wasn't.

I tried to live on my own in that little camper way out in the middle of nowhere for a month, but I just kept getting worse. There came a time when I just couldn't do it anymore, so I ended up staying in a friend's house for a few weeks until I got better.

It's times like this when you want someone to help you. And it's inevitable you'll get sick, unless you're incredibly lucky and in good health.

It's important to have a plan in mind of what you'll do if you get sick or injured. Make your lifestyle as efficient as possible for such times, especially if you're alone, so you can minimize your efforts at taking care of yourself.

You also need a backup plan, which might include having enough cash to get a motel room or, if you're a boondocker, at least enough money to stay in an RV park where you can get help if needed. Even the most hardcore boondockers would be wise to have an emergency fund or place to go.

The problem is, if you're a boondocker, you're often out in the backcountry where it's hard to summon help. We all think we're impervious to such things, but we at least owe it to our pets to have a backup plan.

So, the best bet is to have friends you can call when things happen. Always plan for bad times, even if it's just having cans of chicken soup around or having a good stash of medicinals, like cold medications. It's also important to have a first aid/medicinal kit for your pets. I have a notice in my camper of how many pets I have and any medicines they may take.

What happens if you get really sick, like maybe break a bone or end up in the hospital needing surgery? These things affect you more when RVing than if you have a house, especially if you have pets, as you now need to plan for a place for your animals as well as your own recovery. Of course, things are easier when you're not alone.

You'd be surprised at how helpful people are when you need help. Take their compassion as needed and then pass it forward when you can. The worst part of being sick can be recovering without any help. Take the time to make sure you're never in this position. If you're an introvert, make some good friends. Who knows, they may need your help sometime, too.

The fear of getting sick or injured should not deter you from living the RV life—just be prepared. It's unlikely you'll have anything serious happen, but if you're prepared, you can deal with it more easily.

Work and Money

Books have been written about how to finance the RV lifestyle, but none really tell you in great detail how to do it. It's impossible to lay out a plan that works for everyone, as each person's case is fairly unique. Some people are better at some things than others, and the amount of money required will also vary.

For example, one person might have a great retirement fund and need nothing else, while another is barely getting by on their Social Security and needs to figure out how to supplement it. And if you're too young to have retirement, you'll have to be resourceful and figure out how to survive financially on your own.

Because you already have your rig (hopefully), you won't need as much to live on as if you had a house to maintain and pay for. In fact, this is becoming one of the main reasons people live in RVs—to forego the expense and trouble of having a house.

How much will you need? First, figure out the expenses you incur every month, no matter where you are—things like food and car insurance and clothing. Now add in costs that are associated with your rig, such as insurance (unless you chose to self-insure, which many do) and maintenance.

Add a bit extra for that category, as you'll want to build up a fund for when things break down.

Now, figure out how much your gas will cost, based on how much travel you'd like to do, then double it, as you'll invariably use more than you expected, especially if you like to explore.

Add in some for medical insurance (unless you self-insure, once again) and for potential medical costs for your pets, if you have any. There may be other ongoing expenses you have, so add those in.

This will give you a rough idea of what you need, and it may range from several hundred a month (I know one RVer who lives on less than $500 a month) on up to several thousand. If you boondock, you won't need anything for camp sites, but if you plan to stay in campgrounds, add in a rough monthly fee for that, based on what type of campgrounds you like (private RV campgrounds cost more than state parks, for example).

Now that you have a rough figure of what you'll need, how do you go about obtaining that amount of money every month?

This isn't really that easy to do, even though many will tell you it's no big deal, as you can workcamp or make money via the internet. One of the things that bothers me most is when people say to just go for it and it will all work out, just get your rig and hit the road and you can make it work.

Even though this is exactly how I tend to do things, it may be easier for some than for others to do this, and one really should have a good idea of what options they have before committing. If you can't find work and just end up spending all your money, then you're simply in for a frustrating experience.

So, what options do you have for earning money on the road? Let's examine some of the major ones.

First, the internet offers many possibilities, but the competition there is fierce, so you have to find something you're good at and are willing to dedicate time to. That last thing—dedicating your time to something—is critical, because many think the internet is an easy way to make money.

Anyone I've ever known who did well there was working hard and wouldn't consider it an easy job. And you'll need a reliable computer, skills to use it, and an internet connection (I use Millenicom, which has no contract involved nor hidden fees).

First off, forget such schemes as creating a video that will go viral and make you rich or making enough money from your blog to live on. You can make money with a blog, but it has to be well thought out and offer something others don't. Blogging is a hit and miss financial proposition and usually takes a year or two to catch on, if ever. And even then, you'll be lucky to make a few hundred a month from it. Blogs are often a daily chore, so be sure you're ready to make that commitment. But if you do like blogging, get onto Amazon.com's blogger list as a means of extra income.

Another highly-touted way to make money on the internet is that of writing content for other sites and blogs. This is a possibility, but you'll be competing with many other people, so unless you have a very specialized knowledge base, it's unlikely you'll make enough to live on.

The internet can be a good place to advertise your business, however, and I know a woman who travels all over to pet sit for various people, and her main method for making contact is via her blog: comesitstayfun.blogspot.com

Others have set up Amazon affiliate stores and done well, and still others acquire treasures along the way from yard sales and thrift stores and sell them on the internet, but you do need a place to store such things and a nearby post office or UPS to mail them. And be aware that eBay is not what it used to be as a means for selling, as their fees have gone sky high.

In short, the internet can be a good way to earn cash, but it takes a lot of work and usually a specialized niche. Don't let that discourage you, just be aware it won't be an easy fix to your financial problems.

Some people hit the road thinking they'll make money taking photos and writing about travel for magazines and/or newspapers. This was once a more viable thing, but is now a disappearing proposition as print media becomes more and more scarce.

Probably one of the best ways to make money on the road is via what's called workcamping, or working someplace in exchange for a camp site plus extra cash. Such jobs are typically at private RV parks, and often the pay is low and the work hard. But some people really enjoy this type of lifestyle, as they get to meet people and also be assured of a comfortable place to park their rig for many months at a time.

Some work at Amazon fulfillment centers, which will pay for your RV site while you're working for them, as well as giving you a decent hourly wage. Once again, the work is hard, but if you're in decent shape, it's tolerable. These jobs are usually around the holiday season, and some people make enough doing this to live on the rest of the year.

Another form of workcamper job is being a gate guard. These are typically positions with oil and gas companies. Some people, like my friend above, take caretaking jobs where they can live on site while taking care of animals and pets and even the property of absentee owners.

As RVing becomes more and more popular, there will also be more and more competition for workcamping jobs. There are websites that one can join, usually for a fee, to get the latest listings. Be aware that some employers expect the moon from workcampers. Be sure you understand the position and what's expected of you, as well as the living conditions, before accepting the job.

Campground hosting is another way to ensure having a stable site with hookups without paying for it, but you typically will work for free, although some agencies have a small stipend (typically a few hundred dollars a month). The best way to find these spots is through www.volunteer.gov.

Fortunately, you're typically expected to work part-time when hosting, though some agencies are now asking for more hours as budgets are cut. My personal experiences as a host have generally been positive, but I've heard stories about how poorly some campgrounds treat their hosts. One common complaint is that the parks expect too much.

For more information on hosting, you can read my book, Tales of a Campground Host.

Other methods of making money include creating and selling your art (I know one full-timer who has a silversmith shop in his trailer) or photography at craft fairs. And some RVers work seasonal jobs, saving up enough money to travel again, then repeating the cycle when they run out of funds. I met one RV couple who have a health-care product they developed and now sell at shows, as well as via the internet.

In any case, if you don't have some kind of income and want to be a full-time RVer, expect to be resourceful, but it can be done. And the more frugal you can live, the less time you'll have to spend working and worrying about money.

If you're the type who does like to just jump in and see how resourceful you can be, you'll like the following quote from the actor and voyager Sterling Hayden:

To be truly challenging, a voyage, like a life, must rest on a firm foundation of financial unrest. Otherwise, you are doomed to a routine traverse, the kind known to yachtsmen who play with their boats at sea...cruising, it is called.

Voyaging belongs to seamen, and to the wanderers of the world who cannot, or will not, fit in. If you are contemplating a voyage and you have the means, abandon the venture until your fortunes change. Only then will you know what the sea is all about. "I've always wanted to sail to the south seas, but I can't afford it."

What these men can't afford is not to go. They are enmeshed in the cancerous discipline of security. And in the worship of security we fling our lives beneath the wheels of routine—and before we know it our lives are gone.

What does a man need—really need? A few pounds of food each day, heat and shelter, six feet to lie down in—and some form of working activity that will yield a sense of accomplishment. That's all—in the material sense, and we know it.

But we are brainwashed by our economic system until we end up in a tomb beneath a pyramid of time payments, mortgages, preposterous gadgetry, playthings that divert our attention for the sheer idiocy of the charade. The years thunder by, the dreams of youth grow dim where they lie caked in dust on the shelves of patience. Before we know it, the tomb is sealed.

Where, then, lies the answer? In choice. Which shall it be: bankruptcy of purse or bankruptcy of life?

— Sterling Hayden, from his autobiography,"Wanderer."

Where Can I Park?

Finding a good camp site can be one of the most frustrating experiences around, especially if you're in a bind like my fifth wheeler friend on the 4th of July. It's best to know what's available before you head to a location, but sometimes you just have to go and take what you can find.

Full-time RVers are typically one of three types: those who boondock, those who stay in campgrounds, and those who stay in RV parks on a monthly basis (these may have extensive amenities such as golf courses, pools, and activity centers, as well as extensive prices). The latter tend to attract older retirees, as well as snowbirds, people who go south for the winter, many from Canada.

The boondocker may have the best deal around for campsites, but only if they know the country or are willing to explore it. Most federal lands have rules that allow you to stay in one spot for a maximum of two weeks, so once a boondocker does find a nice area, they can stay awhile, and for free. This refers to designated sites not in campgrounds, which may be so designated merely by some set parameter, such as a previously existing camp spot or a certain maximum distance from the road.

But since most federal lands are in the western part of the country, this can leave one without many alternatives if you're not in the West, and those alternatives usually include staying in a paid campsite. The Army Corps of Engineers does have some holdings, which are a possibility.

Federal lands include the U.S. Forest Service (USFS), the Bureau of Land Management (BLM), the National Park Service (NPS), and the Bureau of Reclamation (BuRec). If you're over 62, you can buy a lifetime pass for $10 that will allow you to camp at any federal campsite for half-price. Most federal campgrounds are very nice and in scenic places, though they tend to not have full-hookups.

State parks are a resource many forget about, but I've found that for the money, they're very much worth it. State parks often aren't far from boondocking in terms of peace and quiet, yet allow you to enjoy showers and trash service, as well as having water. And sometimes, especially during bad weather, it's nice to feel the security of knowing there are others around.

If you're 62 or older, buying an annual state parks pass can be well worth the money, and a season pass allows you the day use of any park in that state, which includes free water and trash. Some states will give season pass holders a discount on camping fees as well. Some will sell passes only to residents, while other sell them to anyone.

Other than paid campgrounds such as KOA, you can stay in truck stops such as Flying J/Pilot, as well as in some Walmart parking lots (ask first). Some businesses, like Cracker Barrel, always welcome RVers. In addition, some towns have municipal campgrounds that aren't typically well-advertised, and some will let you stay at their fairgrounds free of charge.

If you prefer RV parks, it pays to join a membership where you get a discount, such as Coast to Coast, Resort Parks International, or Thousand Trails.

In my mind, one of the best ways to find good camp sites is to read blogs and ask on sites such as RV.net.

Know your vehicle's limitations before going into a spot you might not be able to get back out of, though this is rarely a problem if you have four-wheel drive, although there are times you can't turn around when pulling your trailer.

I read once about a guy pulling a big rig who crossed a one-lane dam, thinking a campground was on the other side. He was misinformed, and there was no place to turn around, so he had to back that big rig all the way across that dam.

The following are a few things to think about when looking at a camp site:

Is there sunlight for your solar?

If it's a hot day, you might want more shade than if it's cool, and you can orient your rig to help keep it at whatever temperatures you desire.

Is the site in a possible drainage basin? If it rains, are you in a wash that can flash flood, or are you near a wall that can slump?

Which way will the wind come if it starts blowing? You'll want to orient your trailer so it has the least possible exposure, especially if high winds are predicted.

Are there close neighbors? Will you disturb their solitude? I can't tell you how many times I've had people camp right next to me when the entire campground is empty.

The following is a good source for free campsites around the country:

http://freecampsites.net

Will I Be Safe?

RVing shouldn't be scary, even if you're alone. There are lots of good people out there who will help you if you need it. The secret is to use common sense. The other secret is to not watch the news on TV, as it distorts everything by focusing on what's sensational.

For example, it's common sense to not camp in sight of a major highway, unless you're in an RV park. The more tucked away you are, the fewer people who will know you're there. Trust your instincts. If a place doesn't feel right, don't try to talk yourself into staying, just move on.

Run a tight ship in case of an emergency. When I go to bed, everything's put away and I always make a point of checking to make sure that if I have to leave in the middle of the night, nothing I can't replace will be left behind. I've only left once in the middle of the night in many years of camping, and that was when a bear came into camp and wouldn't leave. My instincts said to go, so I did.

Most boondocking places really are safe, but how do you know? I always look for places as far off the path as possible, as people seem to be the source of most problems. But in some places, there's more safety in numbers, and it's OK to ask a group if you can join them and camp nearby.

But don't let fear build up into a reason not to go at all. Depending on where you live, you're usually safer out boondocking than at home.

One of the best safety measures you can have is dogs. With dogs, people tend to leave you alone, and it doesn't have to be a big dog. Some people will put a "Beware of Dog" sign in their window, even if they don't have a dog. Conversely, having dogs often results in meeting people who are also dog lovers.

Concealed weapons can also make you feel safer, though usually you're not. A canister of bear spray is probably more effective than a gun, and you're not as likely to die if your opponent takes it from you. In all my years of boondocking, I've never had a need for any kind of weapon, unless you count the pebbles I once threw at a marmot trying to get into my tent.

I always orient my rig for privacy, with the door away from the most likely place for people to show up. I'm careful to not advertise that I'm alone, but I don't go as far as putting out a pair of men's boots or an extra chair, like some do.

My dogs will alert me if anyone comes into the area, and I trust their judgement. If they don't like someone, neither do I. Seeing how people react to dogs is a good judge of character. If they're friendly to the dogs and the dogs like them, I don't worry. It's very rare that my dogs don't like someone, but then it's rare that I ever meet anyone, as I camp way out in the boondocks.

If I find a place I like, I tend to stay put for as long as I can. It can be hassle to move camp, plus it saves on gas.

That's part of the beauty of boondocking—you're out in nature in beautiful spots and relaxed. Moving a lot can leave you frustrated—loading and unloading, looking for a new camp spot, etc. I find that staying put allows me to get to know a place. Though two weeks is the maximum you can stay in one place on Federal land, a lot of people stay longer in areas not patrolled.

Most government agencies have few resources for routing out long-term boondockers, and they tend to patrol the more popular places. Staying longer than the rules say can be a personal choice, though keep in mind that those rules were written to prevent abuse of the land. If you're a good steward and not bothering the wildlife or trashing the place, then camp away, is my own personal philosophy.

But if you get a ticket, that's also your personal responsibility. I've actually left places earlier than I had to because I was worried about my impact—I would see rabbits and squirrels and know I was camped in the middle of their homes. I tend to only spend about a week in one place before I get hitch-itch.

Be aware that if you're boondocking in Arizona, recent developments suggest you may be ticketed for living in the national forest if you're found to be a full-time RVer, even if you're not violating the 14-day rule. It appears that the national forests in Arizona are becoming more and more restrictive and saying that people without physical sticks and bricks homes are squatters, even if they've only been camping for one night. This has become a very controversial thing one should keep their eye on if going to that region. As an aside, you should also educate yourself on

Valley Fever if going to the American Southwest or southern California.

Reams have been written on paper and on internet forums about safety, yet it's rare to hear about anything happening to someone RVing. Maybe this is because RVers tend to be safer, but I think that it's basically because most people will leave you alone.

Safety measures with your propane and refrigerator are important, yet many don't give them a second thought. For example, how many fire extinguishers are in your RV and do you know how to quickly locate and use them in a crisis?

Most RVs use propane for heating and cooking. Propane is relatively safe if you follow certain procedures when dealing with it. Your trailer should have fire detectors, as well as propane and CO detectors, and they should be installed in the proper places.

For example, propane tends to stay low, so a propane detector should be installed in the lower part of your RV's interior. The odds of such detectors saving your life are much higher than any handgun you may carry for intruders.

Insects and animals are pretty low on the hazards list, too, unless you're allergic to bees or wasps or you're camping carelessly in grizzly country (i.e., cooking and making your camp attractive to them).

When I camp in an area with neighbors, I find that going over and talking to them dispels any fears on my part as well as on theirs. Once you talk to someone, the fear of the unknown is gone, and you're likely to have met a new friend. In addition, you can keep an eye out for each other.

Finally, it's best to let someone know where you're at, whether it's a friend or family, especially if you're alone. And those of you who wander a lot may want to get the SPOT Satellite GPS Messenger finder, which can be found on Amazon.com. The service isn't cheap, but it may save your life.

On Loneliness and Civilization

Because they're so happy to get away from everything, beginning RVers tend to underestimate their need for civilization. It's common to crave being out in the middle of some beautiful place, especially when you're in a stressful situation and wanting to get away.

But sometimes we need the comfort of other humans, even if we don't actually talk to them, and it's also good to be close to a town, where you can go and get fresh groceries and be around other people when you want.

I've camped for weeks without seeing another person and start feeling lost and isolated. Sometimes just moving camp makes all the difference, but sometimes I need a people fix.

Boondocking is great for solitude, but don't let solitude turn into true loneliness. The internet can be a good way to stay connected, and reading other RV blogs will give you new ideas of where to go and also help solve problems. Knowing there are many others out there doing what you're doing can help, and sometimes you may even meet up with them.

Many people prefer campgrounds for their social aspects, as well as feeling safer than when they're out on their own. This is fine if you can afford to pay for RV spots, but if you can't, make sure you still find ways to connect to people when you start feeling like an exile.

Of course, we all have different social needs, ranging from needing hardly anyone to needing to be with someone all the time. This varies with different personality types that range from introverted to extroverted. But solo RVers shouldn't fear loneliness, as there are usually more chances to meet people when RVing than when not.

RVing gives you many unique opportunities to meet people from all walks of life. If you're naturally outgoing, it's easy to meet people, especially if you're in a touristy area. It goes without saying, however, that if you hole up out in the boondocks, you may meet hardly anyone.

Even shy RVers can easily meet people if they'll make an effort. You'll meet people in the campgrounds and on the trails, and they'll typically have similar interests to yours. Sitting outside your rig in campgrounds in the evenings is a great way to meet new people, as folks often walk around and say hello to each other.

Workcamping is another good way to meet people, as is campground hosting. Many life-long friendships have started this way, and some will even invite you to come stay at their homes.

If you're not interested in either of these activities, you might consider volunteering at an animal shelter or Goodwill or library in the town nearest you, even if you're only going to be there a few days. Such places are usually happy to get help.

And now that you're mobile, you can go visit family and friends whenever you wish. There's really no reason to be lonely.

Traveling with Pets

One thing that can mitigate loneliness as well as make you feel safer is to have a pet, and many RVers have dogs and cats and even birds.

Dogs are really easy to travel with, as they usually just want to be with you, doing what you're doing. Cats are a bit more tricky in that you have to watch that they can't get out and you also must provide a litter box, but in general they're about as easy as dogs in every other way.

If you have pets, there is no reason you can't RV with them. I have three cats and three dogs with me in my 18-foot trailer, and we all get along fine. I spend a lot of time outdoors with the dogs, and the cats go outside in their little Abo cat tents. One of the cats likes to walk with a leash and harness.

Concessions will have to be made for your pets, things such as keeping them cool and warm, and sometimes you won't go places you'd like for fear of leaving them for too long. I usually take my dogs with me everywhere, as long as it's not too hot for them in my car if I need to run errands, then I'll leave them in my trailer where my AC or Fantastic Fan will keep them cool.

One thing I've found very disturbing during my time as a campground host is when people leave their pets for long periods of time. I can understand this on a very rare basis, but in general, it shouldn't be done. It's not fair to your furry friends to not be a part of your daily activities.

For more information, especially about traveling with cats, read my book, "RVing with Pets."

Communications and the Internet

Once you delve in, you'll find there are as many ways to RV as there are RVs. And you'll also find you're not as alone with any problems that may come up as you may have thought—the internet is a vast archive of questions and answers to about anything that you may ponder or need to know. It can also stave off loneliness and provide a ton of information about where you want to go and what there is to do there.

If you do nothing else, invest in an internet connection when you're on the road. It's an invaluable way to connect with others who understand what you're doing and why.

It's also invaluable for finding things in places you aren't familiar with—things like good boondocking spots and campgrounds, the best place to get that pesky heater fixed, where not to go and where to go to best enjoy your trip, as well as that one concern all RVers always have on their minds—what's up with the weather?

I've RVed without the internet, and the comparison in well-being is off that charts. I'll never be without it again for long, and I'm even a bit of a Luddite.

It also goes without saying that you'll need a cellphone. You may not want an extensive plan, but I guarantee a cell phone will pay for itself over and over in handiness and being able to connect with people when you want. Is the library open today? Just call and save yourself a long drive. Does the local hardware store carry your type of fuses? You get the picture—and your cell phone can be a life-saver, literally, if you have an accident or medical problem.

Ham radio can be well worth the effort and price of getting the license and equipment. Now that the test for Morse code has been eliminated, all one needs to do is study the sample tests on the internet and go take the exam from a local ham club.

A good hand-held radio can be purchased for as low as a hundred dollars. Ham radio provides communications across barriers cell phones can't navigate, especially when cell towers are limited for your region. And it's a fun hobby, one where you can make lifetime friends and relieve boredom and loneliness. And if you have the right kind of ham license, you can even talk to the astronauts on the space station!

Ham radio can also give you the latest in weather and road conditions from hams right in the area, something even the internet can't always do. And hams are famous for their communication assistance in emergencies.

I grew up around ham radio, and it's a lot of fun, and can be the perfect solution to RV communication needs.

Weather

One of the great things about RVing is that you can follow the seasons, going north in the summer and south in the winter. This ensures you a better chance at having good weather most of the time. Many snowbirds have developed life-long friends who all return to the same spot every year.

Even though you may have the internet, a hand-cranked weather radio is an essential as it needs no power. If your power ever fails, you can still find out what the weather will be like.

Watching the weather becomes more than just a hobby when living outdoors, it can mean your very survival. This may seem extreme if you're used to living in a house, but if you're living in an RV, you have to be prepared, as you don't typically have the same kind of secure buffers a house-dweller has. A wind that barely affects a house may blow you into Kansas, though in general most RVs are pretty safe.

Also, knowing the coming weather helps you schedule your day, as in what to store away and whether or not to go get more supplies or even move camp. And knowing the wind direction is important to orienting a rig for safety.

Food and Water

What kind of food you take along depends on whether or not you have a refrigerator. No, not all RVers have or even want refrigerators. I myself prefer the simplicity of not having one, especially since refrigerators are the most frequent source of RV fires. Also, there's no need to be perfectly level if you don't use the frige. I sometimes use my refrigerator for food, and I sometimes use it for storage.

My food supplies on a typical day will include a good organic coffee, and since I like to use milk in it, I buy milk in the little cartons that don't need refrigeration. When that's not available, I'll buy the small cans of evaporated milk. The dogs and cats get what I can't use, so no worry about spoiling.

I eat lots of fruit and veggies that don't need to be kept cool, as well as PBJ sandwiches. I like to juice things and have a blender I can plug into my inverter. Canned soups and breads are good, as well as anything that keeps, like nuts, granola bars, etc.

When I go into town I always buy fresh everything, but only what I can eat in a couple of days. If you're camping in the winter or where it's cool at night, you can store your food outside, always being aware that critters (and bears) may share without being invited.

Just be careful not to become a fast food junkie, which is easy to do if you don't have a frige and don't want to cook much, though it's hard to find fast food if you're not around towns much.

Sometimes I wish I were more of a cook, especially when I'm camping around those who are. These people typically love their friges and couldn't exist without them, as they store all kinds of stuff for their culinary escapades.

Whatever you do, always have lots of water. The more water you can carry, the better, unless you have hookups.

The rule of thumb for drinking water is one gallon per person per day, and add more for washing and cooking. I've found that with about 25 gallons, I can keep myself, three dogs and three cats going for about two weeks. This goes up when it's hot and doesn't include water for showering.

Power

If you stay in campgrounds with full hookups, you'll never have to worry about electricity, but if you boondock or stay in dry campgrounds, you'll soon be dealing with the issue of how to generate power.

One can live without power, but having it makes dealing with the elements much easier. Unless you live in a perfect climate, you'll eventually want to be able to run your heater or your AC unit or fan. There are several methods for doing this, and they all require a certain amount of money to get started.

Some people think generators are the way to go. Often, the larger RVs come with an in-house generator built into the unit, so all you need to do is keep it maintained and carry gas and oil for it. These generators are typically noisy, and carrying gas can be a problem unless you have a pickup, as carrying jerry cans in your rig can be dangerous and messy.

A generator can be used to charge your batteries, or you can plug whatever you want to power directly into it. As a campground host, I once had to ask my neighbors to shut down a generator being used to power a fondu maker at midnight, keeping everyone awake.

Some love the smaller 1,000 watt portable generators like the Honda 1000i and the Yamaha EF1000is, as these can be used to charge your batteries as well as run your computer, as they have pure sine-wave inverters built into them (the kind of inverter that best protects your computer and electronic gear) These generators won't power your air conditioner, as even the small AC units need at least 2500 watts, and some more, as they have a high draw when getting started.

For those times when the generator is not running and producing AC power, a 1000 watt inverter usually provides plenty of power from your charged battery for computers, cell phones, and small appliances.

Solar is the preferred choice of most boondockers, as it's silent and needs no maintenance. Think of your solar panels as a type of battery charger, and as long as your battery already powers your lights and heater blower, you won't need anything else to be a happy camper, as your trailer will already have a converter that makes that electrical charge accessible to your 12 volt appliances.

You can have solar panels attached onto the roof of your rig (or tow vehicle) or purchase portable panels, some which come in suitcases. I personally prefer the portable solar panels because I can orient them to the sun without having to move my vehicle, and if I sell my rig, I can keep them.

If you want to run anything that runs on AC current (and not plug it directly into a generator), you'll need an inverter, which converts your DC power into an AC current, and the wattage needed is determined by what you need to power. Most people who use solar end up getting an inverter, though it's not necessary if you just stick with running what's in your trailer and already hooked up to your trailer battery.

I've found that 90 watts with a 600 watt inverter is about all I need for running my laptop and a few other appliances, as well as keeping the battery charged up enough to run my heater blower at night. I've spent extended periods winter camping with this setup and never had any problems, as long as I had fewer than two or three cloudy days in a row.

You may want to get a larger solar system and add a battery or two to your setup. This will give you a better reserve in case of cloudy weather or if you like to run more stuff. Reserve batteries are great for nights when it's really cold, as the furnace will run more often and wear down the main bank. If you have a slide-out or power jacks, you'll want to keep power in reserve for when you decide to move.

In any case, a number of good companies exist that can help you with solar setups.

Staying Clean

If you're a bit OCD, staying clean might be a bit of a challenge. I like to shower every day, and it's hard not being able to. But you learn to adapt, and things like keeping your hair short and taking a sponge bath can make the lack of showers tolerable. Solar showers are nice if you can spare the five gallons they typically take. I've found that I can wash my hair with about one gallon of water.

If you let your standards slip a bit, it gets easier. By about the third or fourth day, you don't really notice. But when you do get the luxury of a real shower, you feel like you're in heaven. Rec center showers are typically cheaper than those in truck stops or RV parks, and often cleaner. Have a pair of shower shoes (flipflops, Crocs, etc.).

As far as keeping your rig clean goes, that's up to you and how you choose to spend your time, but it's pretty much a losing battle to expect high standards when you're camping in the dirt and elements. The only full-timers I know who have clean rigs are those who always stay in RV parks.

Most full-timers lower their standards a bit, especially when living with pets. You do things like shake things out daily instead of heading to the laundromat all the time. You wear that shirt an extra day or two or even three, depending on if you're around other people or not.

Laundromats can be judged by their general level of cleanliness, though sometimes you have to just use what's available. They can be a good place to check your email and charge up your phone and computer. They can also sometimes be a place to find out about the area and meet people. It did take me awhile to get used to laundromats when I started full-timing, as I'd always had my own washer and dryer.

Except for clothes and bedding, there's not much to keeping a rig clean, especially a small one. Sweep the floor, maybe wash the windows once in awhile, keep the counters clean, and mop occasionally.

Trash is one of the real headaches of RV living. I try to buy things that aren't over-packaged. I also discard all unnecessary packaging immediately after buying groceries, throwing it all away before I even leave town.

In camp, I usually have three trash sacks—one for things I can burn (if I'm in a place that allows campfires), one for things I have to dispose of, and one for things I can recycle. Some towns have made it almost impossible to get rid of trash, locking their dumpsters and threatening one with fines. This is when trash becomes a real challenge, and your creativity has to kick in.

Bathroom facilities can be a problem when you boondock if your rig doesn't have a bathroom. A porta potty is commonly used, and some prefer a bucket, using cat litter to deodorize the scents until it's discarded. Do not bury your waste, as animals typically dig it up and it can be toxic to them, not to mention to other campers.

One of the most essential things you need is lots of water. This allows you to wash frequently, especially your hands. But I think your immune system gets better the more you're outdoors and camping.

It's nice to have a solar shower, and I suggest buying a portable bath-house tent if you're around people much. Be sure to use environmentally friendly soaps, if any at all.

Having an Exit Plan

Something to think carefully about is what you'll do if RV-ing turns out to not suit you, or you have to bail for various reasons, such as health or unforeseen responsibilities (parental care, etc.). Having an exit plan is prudent, even if you're not yet sure how you would execute it.

If you do go ahead and sell your house, you will also lose the ability to move back into it if you decide that full-timing is not the life you had hoped it would be. You'll then have to find a new place to live, which may be difficult, and you may not have the money you need to do that.

This is exactly why some people choose to rent out their homes, typically using a property manager to take care of things while they're on the road. This may be especially hard if you were planning on using the sale of your home to finance your new RV life, which many people do.

One exit plan is to join an RV club that has an RV park that allows you to live in your rig while receiving on-site care. Escapees is one such club, with sites in several places, including Texas, Alabama, Florida, and Arizona. This type of life allows you to share your post-traveling years with like-minded people.

And Finally...

A lot remains that can be said about this special lifestyle, but the best thing for you to do at this point is to determine how badly you want to full-time RV. Look back through the sections in this book about having the casual desire versus really wanting to do it, and whether or not you're the right personality type.

But remember, no one but you gets to determine what your life should be, and even if the odds are against you, you can persevere and do exactly what you want, within reason, of course.

In closing, I've always liked the following quote:

Change only takes place through action. Frankly speaking, not though prayer or meditation, but through action. – the Dalai Lama

May your path be a happy one, whatever direction you may choose.

Afterword

It's an early March morning, and I settle into my patio chair in my long-johns, still half-asleep, sipping strong coffee while watching the sunrise light up the redrock ramparts of Arches National Park in the distance.

A bluejay sits in the juniper tree across from my camp where it's been waiting since before dawn. I toss it a bit of coffee cake, and it quickly swoops down and is gone in a purple-blue flash.

Directly to my east stands a range of 12,000-foot mountains, yesterday's spring storm adding depth to the white cloaks on their tall blue shoulders. It was cold enough last night to freeze my seven-gallon water containers, and frost now slowly melts off the plastic, making small pitter-patter holes in the red sand.

Yesterday evening, as I sat in this same chair, I could see the pale golden light of a distant town reflecting off the clouds. As the night sky opened, I looked overhead into a vault of twinkling stars that reminded me that I'm but a very small part of a vast universe, a feeling that helps keep my simple ambitions in check. Living in the wilds keeps things in perspective.

As the day began in earnest, I did the chores necessary to keep things ticking—feed the dogs and cats and then throw a handful of dog kibble to the pair of ravens who frequent my camp (they're partial to "Taste of the Wild").

I washed up and got dressed, putting on a baseball hat to hide the fact that my hair always stands straight up, then shook out the sleeping bags, swept a few red ants off the outside mat, then made yet more coffee and sat back down to again enjoy the views.

Sometimes, while I'm gazing at all this beauty, I wonder if I'm really still alive. Maybe I died during the night and am now in Paradise. But if that's true, I was in Paradise before I died, since yesterday was just like today.

I quickly come back to reality when I remember how cold I got last night, waking to seeing my breath in the air, even though I was wrapped up in two down sleeping bags with dogs banking my sides. I had finally managed to warm up enough to get to sleep when one of the cats jumped out of her perch on the TV stand above my bed right onto my head, a sensation that's maybe like an earthquake where a soft furry rock falls on you.

There's a lot of hard work that goes into each and every day of living in a little camp trailer out in the desert. You're surrounded by some of the most stunning scenery that exists on Planet Earth, but by the end of each day, you feel like you've paid your dues for all that beauty, as it's a hard life, this life close to the earth—though in other ways, it's an easy life.

Sometimes I hate it, but most other times I love it. It's a lifestyle I have no choice over because I'm hopelessly bound to my freedom—I can't live any other way and be happy. Don't ask me why, it's just how I am, but I believe many others are the same way—I meet them all the time on the road, a whole subculture of nomads, people like me who just want their freedom to go where they want each day, doing exactly what they want.

Maybe you're one of us—a nomad—ready to leave your old life behind, whether by choice or from economic necessity. If so, you can rest assured that getting free won't be easy—it may be the most difficult thing you've ever done—but it will also be the most liberating and rewarding.

I hope this book has helped point you in the right direction, even though once you hit the road, there really is no right direction. You're free to point your wagon wherever you want to go on your own path of freedom.

Welcome to a new way of thinking and living, to a new path and a new life.

—Sunny Skye

One of the gladdest moments of human life, methinks, is the departure upon a distant journey into unknown lands. Shaking off with one mighty effort the fetters of habit, the leaden weight of routine, the cloak of many cares and the slavery of home, man feels once more happy. —Sir Richard Burton

About the Author

Sunny Skye was born in Western Colorado, where her family always went camping, as there wasn't much of anything else to do. She's been RVing all her life, except for time spent going to college and working, and is now an expert on life in the outdoors and the many ways to live well without the amenities of civilization and being in debt.

Sunny now lives full time in her RV with her cats and dogs, campground hosting at various places, spending summers in Colorado, Montana, and Alaska, and winters in Utah.

You'll enjoy her other books, *The Truth About the RV Life, RV Boondocking Basics, RVing with Pets,* and *Tales of a Campground Host.*

And don't forget to check out the books by Sunny's friend, Bob Davidson: *On the Road with Joe* and *Any Road, USA.*

Cover photo by Sunny Skye.

Yellow Cat
PUBLISHING™

Made in the USA
Columbia, SC
11 November 2022